Blessing the Waters

poems by

Angela Griner

Finishing Line Press
Georgetown, Kentucky

Blessing the Waters

*For Love, for Grief,
and those who have been present for all of it.*

Copyright © 2020 by 978-1-64662-298-6
ISBN 000-0-00000-000-0   First Edition
All rights reserved under International and Pan-American Copyright Conventions. No part of this book may be reproduced in any manner whatsoever without written permission from the publisher, except in the case of brief quotations embodied in critical articles and reviews.

ACKNOWLEDGMENTS

There are so many women I am grateful for in my life. The ones that have been with my heart during the season I wrote these words are: my mother, Judy Brady, my grandmothers, Pearl Ford and Jane Talbot and dear friends: Melonie Rosenfarb, Britt Tisdale, Mandy Richardson, Danielle Evans, Stacey Griner, Ginny Celoria, Lauren Sharrett, Misty Brandenburg, Phileena Heuertz, Pat Stark, and Carolyn Kutsko. You know the depths of my struggles. For Stacy Barton, Rosalind Brenner, and Phileena Heuertz, thank you for your kind words in support of these poems. For my boys, Elliot and Isaiah and their grace and magic. I'm forever amazed and grateful to be your mom. For the men and women in 12 step groups I've visited with, your service and friendship have been another lifeline. It is God who heals my life. I'm grateful for all that I know of Love and the ever-increasing mystery and growing uncertainty that causes me to truly live one day at a time. I am thankful for unconscionable grace and goodwill. Finally, I didn't know when I wrote these poems about love, loss, and grief that I would be losing my brother, Aaron Brady, to tragic circumstances. I love you. I miss you and hope your heart is at peace and full of joy.

Publisher: Leah Maines
Editor: Christen Kincaid
Cover Art: Angela Griner
Author Photo: Melonie Rosenfarb of Imago Creative
Cover Design: Elizabeth Maines McCleavy

Order online: www.finishinglinepress.com
also available on amazon.com

Author inquiries and mail orders:
Finishing Line Press
P. O. Box 1626
Georgetown, Kentucky 40324
U. S. A.

Table of Contents

Blessing the Waters 1

Pause. Selah 2

Orlando Summer 3

Blue Heron 4

Mothers 5

Blood & Water 6

My Grandmother Pearl: In Memory 7

Giving Thanks 8

Bless the Space Between Us 9

Prophecy of Hope 10

Fluid 11

I Share My Love with Grief 12

Longings 13

Homecoming 14

Nestling 15

Moonlit Path 16

Prayers for a Son 18

Sing to Me 20

The Goodnight Kiss 21

Bless the Light that Comes Out from the Darkness 22

An Apologetic Elegy 23

Friendship 24

For Isaiah 25

The Snout-Faced Hissing Thing 27

Introduction

These writings have emerged during a season of grief; grief born from stories, personal and from those I love. The stories speak of trauma, old and newly realized, addiction, abuse, loss of innocence, and lost love. They also speak of hope towards redemption and renewal, of consent to solitude, uncertainty, and surrender.

Resurrection will come. That I am certain of. How will it come? What will it finally look like? I haven't a clue.

Blessing the Waters

Bless the hands that turned me away,
the heart that could not be broken again.
Bless the wounds that did not heal,
that have kept the waters barren.

With my lips I bless these hands
and give permission to roam,
to make love,
to find solace.

Bless the hands that ask to love me now,
the heart on the mend.
Bless the wounds that have found their home
and the waters that will flush them out.

Bless the child that could not say no,
the body that could not save him.

Bless the hands that could not hold me
and the ones that hold me now.

Pause. Selah.

Try pronouncing it as something other than good.
Attempt to declare that it isn't vile, pathetic, or wrong. It is what it is. You feel what you feel. You long for what you long for. You grieve for what you must.

Instead, pause a moment. Consider it. Pay attention. Arrest judgment. Move in closer. Try not to run or hide from it. Try not wrestle or struggle either. Just breathe for a moment. Deep. Inside and out.

There are other words that will come, dripping out your pores onto the ground, a slow breeze up through your fingers and hair, tasting it in your mouth. Holy, kind, gentle, honest, from the roots of where it originated from.

Listen, look, give a kind, watchful eye. Then, you can start to name properly. You can start to choose with a knowing, that this is what your heart needs and this is what it doesn't. Selah.

Orlando Summer*

Late afternoon and the soaking foliage
heavy, damp, lively and restless;
The tiny plot with a million oak leaves,
layer upon layer, full of vigor and decay.

The burgeoning tropicals, the insistent weeds,
the anxious parents, the restive children,
the overwrought neighborhood street.
Ambitious fire of noonday sun strengthening
the obstinate, unpredictable sky.

In the midst of all, Grace,
floating like the dandelion seed head,
soaring with the wind over the flattened roof tops;
Flushing out despair with every breath.

Grace with her unconscionable goodwill,
Her determined presence
Her steady tutelage
whispering, whispering
out of the chasm of chaos
out of the stifling heat.

*Homage to Willa Cather's "Prairie Spring."

Blue Heron

Someone lost their mate today
    their child, their mother.
Another's belly is full
    as she drinks of the water.
She cleans herself,
    passersby move cautiously.
She watches me
    watching her.
She doesn't like observers.
I place anthropomorphic shame upon her chest.
I comment on withheld resentment.

Mothers

The dust worn path mothers before us have gone
      softened padded heels
      elephant matriarchs
      pillars founding the land with every step

We know this country
      this burnt earth fire valley
      echoing green, warm hearth traveling
      by city, sea, and valley

Within us
      young girls are bent over dewy grass
      tomorrows toes massaging, awakening dark earth
      beckoning wild fires into their hands
      releasing them into the night sky
      cornucopias of light

Blood & Water

Let the red blood and water soak you through.
Let the rage come up, over flood, over fill.
Then, bring up the fire, rolling, tumbling through you, smothering the resistance.

Let the wound, the love, and the passion live and be open-
mingled together-enmeshed.
Yes, pain, hurt, rage, loving tenderness, softness-
fire and water and blood and bone and flesh,
all rise up and meet you.

Stretch out your arms.
Open up your chest and scream out with all you have,
"You are welcome here! Take it all."

You will be consumed at once and reborn-remade-renewed. The fire and the breaking and the ashes are the parts of the whole healing thing.

Cry out. Scream out. Let it all come gushing, crushing, crashing down.
In these sands and ashes, you will retire and renew, at once-together.

Give in.
Give it up.
Grant it all you have,
or else,
when this is all said and done
you will be only a shell of yourself
and we are not for that.

We want all of you:
here,
present,
whole.

My Grandmother Pearl: In Memory

She is Tennessee country and Ohio hills
southern comfort and wild will
gold and silver with Queen Anne's lace
the weeping hour holding space
interceding on our behalf
a country road, a quiet path

She is maple syrup in slow motion
the tree that offers the magic potion
flowing down the splintering bark
to soothe the soul and nourish the heart
honey on biscuits, with gravy too
a crowded table on a Sunday afternoon
bacon grease, beans, casserole and potatoes
cookie sheets, wax paper, and garden tomatoes

The bumble bee, the hummingbird
blue eggs in robin's nest
the trees that hold them, the rubied chest
the bright wings that fly and the muted ones that hold
young ones in need of comfort and fledglings on the road

She is a song to be sung and the singer that sings
praises immortal on guitar strings
She is blue grass and cherry wine
the gospel hour on Sunday's time
a church pew padded with her people
hallelujah's rising out beyond the church steeple
bright shining sun over ten thousand hills
grace that brought our hearts to heal

A mending, bending, intertwining love
She is the olive leaf and the dove
a gilded painting of roses in oil
a prophetic word to calm your sorrow
the glinted, sparkling leaf
over a river, a cold relief
on a warm summer's day in Tennessee light
the cool moonlit grass of Ohio's gentle night

Giving Thanks

Gratitude stains my hands
and licks my open wounds
sets my heart to a blood pumping rhythm

calls to a native joy to come up
alongside the savage beast of my pain

helps me breathe in and bleed out
both blood and breath a burning, stinging, salve

I cannot live spitting the blood of bitter rage
(Of course, that too is a salve-a temporary relief-a razor-blade-band
aid creating more wounds and scars on application.)

Gratitude is the hard, heavy, way
the muscle-building, aching way-
that clears the senses
opens the wounds
for finished healing
raises up the native joy
to tame the wild beast

Bless the Space Between Us

Bless the space between us
the wrenching a part place
the coming together place
the yearning space
the hope for tomorrow space

the sacred space of possibilities
the place where no one has yet to claim
the room for new beginnings
the room for leaving

the thin lines to mark our souls to make our own way
the permeable lines where we can fall in, to comfort one another

the restoring place for grounding and wisdom
the healing place where we do no harm
the stepping out place
the going back in space

Bless the space between us
and the surrender of coming home
wherever that may be

Prophecy of Hope

One day I will tell you the story of our love
and it will be whole
It will always have been whole

You will remember and re-remember as a part of your redemption

Time will remake itself and you with it
Your love with it will be remade and retold,
all over again

It will be old and new
nascent and wise
all at once

Winter, spring, summer, and fall will rejoice
and intermingle

You will be golden, verdant green
and at rest simultaneously
living
dying
being

Fluid

I am fluid
water rushes
out, within, and through
my veins
my blood
my hands
grief-air and light
love-heavy and destructive

I agree to them all
I consent
I will become
the river
and the ocean
I will ebb and flow with the waves that will come
I will invite them in to stay as long as they must
as long as they choose

I will breathe in the water
the joy
the sadness
the grief and the love
for I will be peace
I will bear hope
I will breathe life as I accept death
I will exhale
the hate with my anger
as it rises
I will let it rise

mountains and oceans are birthed
from this light
this way
this water
this likeness
and all there is
shall be
ever was
evermore
whole

I Share My Love with Grief

What does it mean if what I write makes me cry?
Speaks to me of the acceptance I've yet to grasp,
tells me of the hope that one day I will?

Grieving, grieving, and more grieving.
All I write contains the word,
the flesh of it on my bones.
But this is the season.
I need not apologize for what is,
what must be,
so that I might live.

I share my love with grief.
I share my joy with grief.
They nestle together in the chambers of my heart.
I am willing to pay the price.
I cannot bear with less;
Less truth,
less reality,
less love,
less of all things
good, noble, and true.

Longings

I want to know and be known
by the old elm and oak trees,
by the river or the stream,
on the path.
I want to know the path
and the path to know me.

Homecoming

I once was lost
and here I am found
on a beach
at the gulf.
My love is here,
god is within, without.

I am grounded and grounding in the sand,
breathing in the fresh air-
the sea salt scallop ocean creature air.

Welcome, welcome back!
Welcome always!

The blue heron and the many species of birds walk by,
a living scene, a walking stage.
I want to know their names, each one,
the way Oliver knows her streams
and Berry knows his trees.

They also know them.
The streams know her.
The trees know him,
and here, the ocean knows me.

Nestling

Sweet sweat smell of newborn cub
rooting to breathe in the rosy silvery dark

A small child under fresh sheets fanning air
parachuting out gently lighting down
breath & giggles

The fading larva twisting into her long retreat, loosening
herself into her first surrender

I lean into you
an inquisitive push
punctured air
nasal to neck
lips to brow
to nose
to neck

Rolling in tightly
Armadillidium
fluvial, aeolian
breath and air
wind and water

We become compressed molecules
stores for the peaked load
of outer air, shrinking time and
measured tasks

This is sabbath for the body
a balm for the heart
quiet for the mind this
inner solitude shared

A young girl's loose braid in fine strands
is this coming togetherness with easy release
the kind of blissful falling that gives us life
restful slumber
hopeful present
cadenced surrender

Moonlit Path

There is a moonlit path
waiting for you under the shade of the maple tree
in the cooled grass and earth

In the dark
shadowed halos outline
the trees and garden plants
neighborhood lights flicker on
and off dogs barking in the distance
teens running and laughing on
the sidewalk

But you are here
in your grandmother's house
back garden in view from the kitchen sink
between the sliding doors
afraid to stay in
afraid to go out

You venture slowly onto the faux wooden planks
you tuck yourself into a patio chair
keeping a safe distance from the tree
and the dark
and the shadows
all the objects you can no longer make out
tiny infinity symbols imprint the side of your thigh
Slowly you make your way
peel off of the chair
feel the beginnings of your long descent
your back with a slight ache
slows your uprising
passing gently, softly in the green

You lie down
under the tree
you spread your arms out
you are Christ on the cross

spread out in remembrance of the crucible
what has been lost and what has been found

Gentle surrender with trembling heart and hands
in the dark earth begging creatures away
you lie there as long as you can stand it
until heart outlines float up from you
vapor rings passing through the branches and leaves

Dispersing high above
tiny molecules of asks, longings, uncertainties
prayer is your surrender
your surrender is the prayer

Prayers for a Son

Scorching sun rising in the heat
your ruddy cheeks bristle beneath the sheets
    set with eyes cold and gray
    mournful, deep bellowing up from your bowels

howling, aching for reprieve from the
nightmarish struggle
    machinations exceeding
    an unending explosive expanse

reprieve, an illusion
    a swollen river whose bed is dried
    scorched earth
comfort too, illusive
    scorched hearth
resolve and hope
    disparate and receding

You are desperate to be hidden
    within a long slumber
    yet remain a sleepless
    tender beast

Won't light call you out?
Cannot loving hands cajole?

I am a mother's chest full of exhale
    a ribbon bending, winding, moving to find her
    mark to bind the wound and heal the ancient
    arch of Time's regress, but alas, the planted
    honeysuckle's blooms are delayed

The tender owl is held aloft in the night
    her fledglings hungry
    lay waiting.

Merciful father come quickly!

The land is barren.
    Where is the water and the manna?
    The fiery cloud, the corrugated rock?

May this sweet young one lying restless
    wake with a lions' spread, to grow strong
    with David's bow and Jonathan's waiting
    sorrows held
    full with life's bread, honey, and cider

Come out young one with the wild waiting
    for there are leaves gleaming in cool summer
    streams over rocks on craggy hills in the vast
    expanse of land and sea

The serpent's head is crushed.
    The alligator's mouth is clenched.
    The heron's stomach empty.

You are untapered ribbon
    unbound body
    healed Achilles' heel
    Atlas unburdened
    Percy's open quest

Can you see how the fledglings fly into Acropolis?
    transfigured light
    out of the factories of automatons into
    the delicious green of after earth
    out of cathedralled tombs, into clear pools
    in this reign of sun

Sing to Me

Sing to me a song of reconciliation
sing my name
sound it out
recompense
make way through these stars
unearth
unbend
unbreak
and mend

The Goodnight Kiss

Lips, rippled wax, softened from the heat
   stumbling towards the moist pillowed pink
   falling into the cavernous waves of warmth and
   wetness

Breathing you in and out
   my body bends towards you
   a tree bearing the weight of child's play
   a sea storm splitting me wide open
   seedlings awake with the unleashed rays
   falling upon the earth

Bless the Light that Comes Out from the Darkness

How to hold as loosely to the dark
as I do the light?

Love is perfected in loss and longing
and joy is born of pain.
How can this be,
that there is no other way?

I may pretend.
I may not be ready.
I may ask the cup to pass from me.

But it will always come back,
offering itself,
along with
the light that comes after.

Do not worry if you are still pretending.
When we are ready, we will know.
When we are ready, we will surrender.

Then, we will bless the light that comes out from the darkness.
The darkness we thought we could not bear.

An Apologetic Elegy

Here lies the hermit crab from Montauk,
plucked from his homeland,
the pebble rock beach
with the pink sand.

Unknown to his assailant
what crime she had committed,
until miles later
through car, plane,
she discovers her mishap,
her murderous ignorance.

The blow was great.
The Aquatic Creature could not save him.
No sand, shell, or rocks from his homeland could replicate the life blood he needed:
The climate,
the richness,
the breeze.

Nothing could give him back the home he lost.
Dying of a broken heart in the hands of my son as the
clerk at the aquatic center pronounced, "He's gone".

I'm sorry dear Montauk, captive, companion.
I am eternally sorry for my ignorance which tore you
from your home and brought you here in the Tennessee
suburbs to die.

Rest in peace dear creature from Montauk.
May you find glittery shores on which to roam, rest,
move, and have your being restored in the hereafter.

Friendship

Speak the words like honey to remind me of the truth
that I knew yesterday that you needed to hear
today I have forgotten it
tomorrow you may forget again and I will remember
we have each other
we hold the other

For Isaiah

Talk to me and easy laughter
These are the things I was made for,
or I've been recently made over for.

Talk to me about the random things on your mind and
the simple things that make you giggle.
I now know the thing that brought my mother to say I
was her sunshine.

Your cackling around the corner of the house as I pulled
you in with the hose, was a salve to my heart,
my swollen, beating, wounded heart.

Your run from behind the front of the school bus, down
the slope and across the yard.
Your Captain America jacket
half way on and half way off,
flying out with your hair.

You rustle into the door throwing off your things and
expecting attention.
You're home.

A snack? "Look at my papers from today, mommy, a
show, can I just watch a show? A Wild Kratts?"

You want more and more shows but I want to be a good
mom and call you out to playing or doing something
else, less "mushy gushy" as we call it.

You slide onto my lap, with your little body that's grown
almost twice the size in just this past year.

You are so content with such simple things and I am
washed anew by it.
You make me new.
You made me new when you entered this world and my

heart swelled past my body.

It is pure joy you've brought to me,
just simply by being.
Your tender heart,
your wild ways,
you're mine.
For now, I get to call you mine.
And my hands hold that "mine-ness" loosely.
How long? Forever? A moment?

Today's moment of cackling was a forever one.
How did I get to be the lucky one
with all I've been so ignorant of,
all I've tried to keep tight and that has withered,
all I've demanded and expected and felt entitled to?

How did all of that not keep me from this joy?
I'm standing here, in this contemplative stance,
paused in the moment of your laughter
and it is the closest part of heaven
to be seen or heard of on this earth:
Your unbidden,
easy laughter.

The Snout-Faced Hissing Thing

She watches
as the snout faced hissing thing prepares her nest
and the blue gray cat is laid to rest
one home is made in this safe space
while another succumbs to keep the pace

Newness slows to mark its way
herons run against dismay
rough edges smooth
as some memories remove

Still, the old foundation is breaking
her heart feels up for the taking
laid upon the table of a borrowed lot
won by the sweaty handed despot

A mother's calf is bleating
hard won by wolves retreating
eggs and sea creatures scattered about
inside seagull's and crustacean's bloated mouths
light fins in oceans beguiled
and this, this is the mercy wild?

The duckling nestles in the feathered chest
a mother watches, her body at rest
surrendered to the knowing of a secret kept
unfolding just now as her children slept
peacefully, longingly, cautiously bidden
into the unfurling mystery no longer hidden

She nods to the soft-shelled mother laying her eggs
sharing the hope that tomorrow begs
pays homage to the cat and demolished house
returns to her own new offerings espoused

Loves dies quickly and rises swiftly
clutching no thing in talons sickly

release, upend, lay out
display, array, unmount
the wind dies down without regret
blessing the chick and the hungry egret

Angela Griner has worked in the field of education for more than 20 years, with a passion for literature and writing for young children, and inspiring adults to tap into their own creativity to teach young ones the love of reading and writing. She holds an MA in Reading and EdD in curriculum and instruction, specializing in urban and multicultural education. Much of her work in teaching and writing is infused with practices she has learned from contemplative writers and therapeutic work towards emotional healing and wholeness. She is an advocate for mental health awareness and practice throughout all vocations.

She currently resides in Orlando, Florida, with her two sons, husband, and dear friends, teaching, writing, and painting. For more information or permission to use any of the words here, email: angelagriner@gmail.com. To see art work and regularly posted writings see @angelagrinerart on Instagram.

www.ingramcontent.com/pod-product-compliance
Lightning Source LLC
LaVergne TN
LVHW041510070426
835507LV00012B/1474